WINNING LIFE LIKE A WARRIOR

AN INNER SOUL

SANANSHIKA MALIK

Made with ♥ on the Notion Press Platform
www.notionpress.com

This book is dedicated to all those who dare to dream, to grow, and to overcome. To the warriors within each of us who face life's challenges with courage, resilience, and hope. May you always find strength in the darkest moments, and may you continue to rise, no matter how many times you fall.

To my loved ones—who have supported, inspired, and believed in me when I had doubts. Your unwavering faith has been my anchor, and this book is as much yours as it is mine.

And to those who feel lost or uncertain: may this book be a reminder that you are not alone, and that within you lies the power to change your life.

This is for you.

Contents

Contents

Gurupaa

SHUKRANA GURUJI BLESSINGS ALWAYS GURUJI *OM NAMHA SHIVAYE SHIVJI SADA SAHAYE OM NAMHA SHIVAYE GURUJI SADA SAHAYE*

Foreword

The lessons here are not meant to be read and forgotten—they are meant to be applied. The strength of a warrior is not something you simply read about; it is something you live, breathe, and embody every single day. It is in how you rise when you fall, how you respond when faced with adversity, and how you choose to show up for yourself and for the world around you.

So, I encourage you to dive into these pages with an open heart and an open mind. Let the wisdom within guide you, challenge you, and inspire you. And as you move forward, remember this: You are a warrior. You have everything within you to face whatever life brings, and you have the power to emerge stronger, wiser, and more resilient with every battle you fight.

This is your journey. And it begins now.

Preface

I wrote this book because I believe that within each of us lies an untapped source of strength, wisdom, and resilience—a warrior's spirit waiting to be awakened. It's easy to feel defeated when life becomes difficult, but I have come to understand that our most significant growth happens during the hardest times. We are shaped and defined by the battles we fight, and how we choose to fight them.

This book is not about offering quick fixes or easy answers. It's not about teaching you to avoid pain, fear, or failure. Rather, it's about teaching you how to navigate those experiences with strength, grace, and unwavering determination. It's about finding meaning in your struggles, and discovering how you can use them as stepping stones to something greater.

Acknowledgements

Writing a book is never a solitary endeavor, and this work would not have been possible without the support, guidance, and encouragement of many wonderful individuals. I would like to take a moment to express my heartfelt gratitude to everyone who has been part of this journey.

First and foremost, I want to thank my family and my parents (MR.SANDEEP MALIK & MRS.ANSHU MALIK) ,my dearest little sister MS. MEDHAVI MALIK who always encourage me to write this book, my loved ones for their unwavering support and understanding who has been my rock, always believing in me and to my illustrator of this book MR. ROHAN LODIWAL who illustrate me every deep thoughts of warrior .

A special thank you to [mentor/teacher /School (INDERPRASTHA CONVENT SR.SEC SCHOOL, DELHI)], whose wisdom, insights, and advice have been invaluable throughout this process. Your belief in my vision and your guidance at every step has been truly instrumental.

To my editor and writing team, your expertise, keen eyes, and dedication have made this book what it is. Thank you for your constructive feedback, attention to detail, and support in shaping these words into something meaningful.

I am also deeply grateful to the readers—whether you are picking up this book for the first time or returning to it again and again. Your time and attention are precious, and I hope that this work resonates with you and provides value on your own journey.

To everyone who has been part of my personal and professional growth, thank you for your encouragement, inspiration, and love. Every person who crossed my path, whether directly or indirectly, has left a lasting impact on the creation of this book.

Finally, I would like to express my deepest gratitude to the universe for guiding me to this moment, and for providing me the opportunity to share my thoughts and ideas with you.

With heartfelt thanks,
[SANANSHIKA MALIK]

Prologue

This book is an invitation. An invitation to see life as a warrior sees it not as something to endure, but as something to conquer. It's about facing adversity with courage, embracing failure as a teacher, and recognizing that each moment, no matter how difficult, is a chance to grow stronger.

Throughout these pages, you'll find ideas, reflections, and practices that can help you harness your inner power and face life's challenges with unwavering focus. We'll explore how to cultivate resilience in the face of hardship, how to develop a mindset that thrives in the midst of adversity, and how to live a life that is not defined by the obstacles in our way but by the victories we claim over them.

About Author (sananshika Malik)

Hello, and welcome!

I'm Sananshika Malik , and it is both an honor and a privilege to be the author of this book. My journey has been one of discovery, growth, and transformation—one that I am excited to share with you. Like many of us, I have faced obstacles, doubts, and moments of uncertainty in my life. But through it all, I have learned the power of resilience, the importance of mindset, and the transformative strength that comes when we face life as warriors.

There were moments in my life when I felt lost, unsure of my path, or overwhelmed by the weight of the challenges ahead. However, through these trials, I found that my strength was not just in my ability to overcome difficulties but in my mindset—the way I chose to see challenges, the way I approached adversity, and the way I refused to back down in the face of obstacles.

The concept of "winning life as a warrior" came to me as I navigated my own struggles. It became clear that life is not just about surviving; it's about thriving in the midst of hardship, turning pain into power, and using every experience as an opportunity to grow. This book is an embodiment of that philosophy—the culmination of everything I've learned along the way.

As a writer, my goal has always been to help others tap into their own strength, cultivate resilience, and unlock their true potential.

Through this book, I share the tools, mindset shifts, and strategies that helped me rise above adversity. I believe deeply that we all have a warrior spirit within us, and that the battles we face in life are not meant to break us, but to build us into something stronger.

I am forever grateful to the people, experiences, and challenges that have shaped me into who I am today. They have taught me that life is a journey, and while it may not always be easy, it is always worth the fight.

Thank you for taking the time to read this book. I hope the words here inspire you, challenge you, and encourage you to stand strong in the face of life's inevitable struggles. You are a warrior, and you are capable of more than you know.

CHAPTER ONE

INTRODUCTION TO - LIFE

Our life is as equal as butterfly cycle. we come as a form of egg in life and slowly we grow as an adult.
life is a pure version of butterfly. we live,breath,fight,got failed and in end we win as a warrior.

The deep meaning of life is a question that has puzzled philosophers, spiritual leaders, and thinkers also.
While the answer may vary depending on one's beliefs, experiences, and perspective, such as -

1. Connection: Life's meaning can be found in relationships—how we connect with others, share love, and build communities. Our bonds with people, nature, and the world around us help shape our purpose.

2. Growth and Transformation: Life is about evolution—spiritual, emotional, and intellectual. Through challenges, struggles, and triumphs, we learn, adapt, and become more attuned to who we are and who we can become.

3. Purpose and Contribution: Many find meaning in contributing to something larger than themselves, whether that's through helping others, advancing knowledge, or making a positive impact on the world. Our sense of purpose often comes from creating value and leaving a legacy.

4. Experience and Presence: Life's meaning can be found in the richness of the present moment. Through mindfulness and appreciation of simple joys, we can find a deep sense of fulfillment in simply *being*, rather than constantly seeking.

5. Existential Meaning: Some believe that meaning is self-created—that we are the ones who imbue our lives with purpose through the choices we make. In this view, life is not inherently meaningful, but rather, we create meaning through our actions, values, and passions.

6. Spiritual Fulfillment: For many, the meaning of life is tied to spiritual or religious beliefs, such as seeking enlightenment, understanding divine purpose, or aligning with a higher power.

Ultimately, the deep meaning of life is often a blend of personal discovery and collective experience—it's something that each person must explore and define for themselves.

For me, life is where I learn alot things, I cry alot, I failed many times, iI pass , SOMETIMES gave up too. But at the and I
come as a warrior.
With my experiences and exploring a life I can say that a person who learn from thier failure and try to improve
themself will never get failed in any situation.

Lets read the stages of life where we grow towards the calmness.

CHAPTER TWO

STAGE -1 (THOUGHTS)

It all started with thoughts.

Thoughts are the mental processes or cognitive events that occur in our minds, ranging from simple ideas to complex reflections.
They are the way we interpret and make sense of the world around us, shaping our perceptions, beliefs, emotions, and actions.
Thoughts can be conscious, where we actively focus on them, or subconscious, influencing us without our awareness.

we create our destiny through our thoughts. We have many types of thoughts- mental thoughts, general thoughts , problem solving thoughts etc.
But if we talk about main types of thoughts ,then they are only two types will be present.

1. Positive
2. Negetive

The way we think can significantly influence our well-being and actions.

1. Positive Thought -

They help foster a sense of hope, confidence, and resilience and they will boost up your motivation with help of positive thought we may encourage our self better.

Examples of Positive Thoughts:

"I can handle this challenge and grow from it."
"I am grateful for the opportunities I have."
"Mistakes are a part of learning; I can improve."
"Things will get better with time and effort."

2. Negetive Thought-

They can create feelings of doubt, fear, and helplessness, and sometimes lead to unproductive behaviors.it will lead to many harmfull changes in ones behaviour.

Examples of Negative Thoughts:

"I always mess things up; I'll never succeed."
"Things are never going to improve."
"I'm not good enough for this."
"Everything is going wrong, and nothing will ever change."

THOUGHTS CREATE Impact on Life:

Positive Thoughts help build resilience, foster a sense of well-being, and improve problem-solving abilities.
They lead to better mental health, improved relationships, and greater overall satisfaction in life.
Negative Thoughts can lead to stress, anxiety, depression, and feelings of helplessness.
Over time, they can limit personal growth and create barriers to happiness and success.

Changing Negative Thoughts:

It is majorly important to change our negative thoughts from our life. yes, it is difficult but not impossible. changing that thought will give us a better version of our life and
we emerge as a string and motivated person.

Therapy we can do for changeing a negetive thought;-

1. Identify Negative Thoughts

The first step is to become aware of your negative thoughts. Often, they happen automatically and without conscious awareness. Start by noticing when you're feeling stressed, anxious, or down—this is usually a sign of negative thinking.

Example:
If you think, "I always mess up. I'm not good at anything," recognize that as a negative thought.

2. Challenge and Question the Thought

Once you identify a negative thought, ask yourself whether it's true or based on assumptions, exaggerations, or distorted thinking patterns. Common cognitive distortions include:

Overgeneralization: "I failed this time, so I'll fail every time."

Example:
Instead of thinking, "I always mess up," challenge it with, "I've made mistakes before, but I've also succeeded at things. This is just one setback, not a reflection of my overall ability."

3. Reframe the Thought

Reframing means finding a more balanced or positive way of looking at a situation. Instead of focusing on what's wrong, look for what you can learn from it or what you can appreciate about it.

Example:

Negative thought: "I failed the test. I'm dumb."
Reframed thought: "I didn't do well this time, but I can learn from my mistakes and do better next time."

4. Practice Self-Compassion

Instead of being overly critical of yourself, treat yourself with the same kindness you would offer a friend.

Negative self-talk often stems from a lack of self-compassion.
Practice speaking to yourself gently and recognizing that everyone makes mistakes.

Example:
When you make a mistake, instead of thinking, "I'm worthless," try, "I made a mistake, but that doesn't define who I am. I can try again."

CHAPTER THREE

STAGE -2 (CHALLENGES)

Life is a constant ebb and flow of challenges. At one point or another, each of us encounters difficulties that push us to our limits—whether they come in the form of personal setbacks, career obstacles, emotional struggles, or external circumstances that seem beyond our control. These challenges are inevitable, but how we respond to them is what defines us.

Challenges in life are often viewed negatively—something to avoid, resist, or escape. But what if we changed the way we think about challenges? What if we saw them as opportunities for growth, transformation, and strength? The truth is, challenges are not roadblocks; they are stepping stones on the path to becoming who we are meant to be.

1. Personal Struggles

Internal challenges, such as self-doubt, fear, or low self-esteem, are among the toughest battles we face. These are the battles that often go unseen by others but can have the most significant impact on our lives. Overcoming negative thoughts, limiting beliefs, or unresolved emotional pain requires self-awareness, self-compassion, and a willingness to change.

How to overcome it:

Practice self-compassion and affirmations. Speak kindly to yourself as you would to a friend.

Seek professional help if necessary—therapy, coaching, or support groups can provide tools to heal and grow.

Cultivate mindfulness or meditation practices to help quiet the mind and reduce negative self-talk.

2. Health and Physical Challenges

Health challenges, whether physical or mental, can feel overwhelming and isolating. Whether it's dealing with a chronic illness, recovering from an injury, or managing mental health struggles like anxiety or depression, these challenges require a unique kind of strength.

How to overcome it:

Focus on small, incremental changes rather than expecting rapid transformation.

Build a support system of people who understand and encourage your journey.

Learn to listen to your body and honor its needs. Balance rest, activity, and nutrition.

3. Financial Setbacks

Financial struggles are one of the most stressful challenges many people face. Whether it's dealing with debt, unemployment, or struggling to make ends meet, money-related problems can affect every aspect of life and cause anxiety about the future.

How to overcome it:

Take a practical approach: assess your financial situation, make a budget, and cut unnecessary expenses.

Educate yourself about money management and seek out financial advice or counseling if needed.

Stay focused on long-term goals. While short-term struggles may feel heavy, remind yourself that financial situations can improve with time, planning, and persistence.

4. Career and Professional Challenges

Whether it's feeling stuck in your job, dealing with workplace conflicts, or facing unemployment, career-related challenges are common. These challenges can feel particularly disheartening because they directly impact your sense of purpose and identity.

How to overcome it:

Evaluate your career path and determine if you're aligned with your passions and strengths. Sometimes a change is necessary for growth.

Network with others in your field, seek mentorship, and never stop learning. Every challenge can be an opportunity to grow your skillset.

Cultivate patience. Career success doesn't always happen overnight. Stay consistent and resilient, even when it feels difficult.

5. Loss and Grief

Loss is one of the most profound challenges in life. Whether it's the death of a loved one, the end of a relationship, or the loss of a dream or opportunity, grief can feel all-consuming. It's a process that requires time, acceptance, and deep emotional work.

How to overcome it:

Allow yourself to feel the emotions associated with loss. Don't suppress grief, but let it flow through you.

Seek support from friends, family, or a counselor. Grief is often easier to bear when shared with others.

Honor the memory or significance of what you've lost, while also learning to embrace new possibilities for the future.

6. Relationship and Social Struggles

Navigating relationships can be one of the most challenging aspects of life. Whether it's dealing with conflict in personal relationships, loneliness, or a lack of meaningful connection, the emotional toll can be significant.

How to overcome it:

Open communication is key. Practice active listening and honesty in your relationships.

Take responsibility for your part in any conflict. Relationships require mutual effort and understanding.

Focus on building a healthy support system of friends, mentors, and community members. Having strong social connections can provide a buffer against loneliness and emotional stress.

7. Uncertainty and Fear of the Unknown

Life is full of uncertainties. Whether it's fear about the future, making a major life change, or venturing into the unknown, uncertainty can create a lot of anxiety. It's natural to feel fear when facing the unknown, but

it's important to learn to navigate that fear instead of allowing it to control you.

How to overcome it:

Focus on the present moment. Worrying about the future can prevent you from taking the necessary steps today.

Break down big decisions into smaller, manageable steps.

Trust yourself. Believe that you have the capacity to adapt and overcome, regardless of the outcome.

CHAPTER FOUR

STAGE-3 (EMOTIONS)

Emotions are complex psychological and physiological responses to the events, people, or situations we encounter in life. They are an essential part of human experience, influencing our thoughts, behaviors, and interactions. Emotions help us navigate the world by signaling what is important to us—whether that be something to pursue, avoid, or address. They also provide insight into our values, desires, and beliefs.

The Role of Emotions in Life:

1.Survival and Adaptation: Emotions like fear and anger have evolved to help us respond to immediate threats, ensuring survival. For instance, fear alerts us to danger, while anger can provide the energy needed to confront a threat.

2.Decision Making: Emotions can guide decision-making by influencing how we evaluate choices. Positive emotions may lead us to approach a situation, while negative emotions may cause us to avoid it.

3.Social Connection: Emotions are central to forming relationships and social bonds. For example, love and empathy foster close relationships, while feelings of jealousy or guilt can affect social dynamics and help us understand and manage interpersonal conflict.

4.Self-Understanding and Growth: Emotions often provide insight into our inner world, highlighting what matters to us, what we value, and where we might need to grow. By reflecting on our emotions, we can gain greater self-awareness and work toward emotional growth.

5.Communication: Emotions often serve as non-verbal signals to others. For example, body language and facial expressions can convey happiness, sadness, anger, or surprise, helping others understand how we feel and what we need.

How Emotions Affect Well-Being:

1.Positive Emotions: Happiness, joy, and contentment can promote mental and physical well-being. They enhance resilience, reduce stress, and contribute to better overall health.

2.Negative Emotions: While negative emotions like sadness, fear, or anger can be distressing, they are not inherently harmful. They serve important functions, such as signaling that something needs to change or that a goal is not being met. However, when negative emotions are prolonged or suppressed, they can lead to mental health challenges like anxiety or depression.

Emotional Challenges:

1.Emotional Overwhelm: Some individuals may feel overwhelmed by intense emotions, especially if they lack the tools or support to process them. This can lead to burnout, anxiety, or emotional breakdowns.

2.Suppression or Avoidance: Trying to ignore or suppress emotions can lead to long-term negative consequences, such as emotional numbness or unresolved emotional issues.

3.Emotional Dysregulation: In some cases, such as in certain mental health conditions like borderline personality disorder or depression, emotions can be difficult to regulate, leading to mood swings, impulsive behaviors, or difficulty maintaining relationships.

-Emotions are an integral part of the human experience, offering valuable insights into our internal world and guiding our actions and decisions. While they can sometimes be difficult to manage, emotions are ultimately a source of strength, creativity, and connection. Developing emotional intelligence—understanding, expressing, and regulating emotions—can lead to greater mental well-being, healthier relationships, and a more fulfilling life.

Improving negative emotions is an important part of emotional health and well-being. While negative emotions like sadness, anger, fear, and frustration are a natural part of life, learning how to manage and transform them can prevent them from becoming overwhelming or long-lasting.

CHAPTER FIVE

STAGE -4 (FAILURE)

Failure in Life is often viewed as a negative experience, but in reality, it can be one of the most transformative and valuable aspects of personal growth. Failure is not the end of the road, but a stepping stone toward success, learning, and self-improvement. It provides opportunities to reflect, recalibrate, and continue moving forward with greater wisdom.

failure refers to the inability to meet a desired goal or expectation. It can manifest in many forms:
not achieving a career goal, experiencing a setback in a relationship, facing financial struggles,
or even failing to live up to one's own standards. However, how we respond to failure is what truly matters.
Having a failure feeling in life can led many traumas.

We humans think that a fail person can NOT do any thing in their life. They must be nOt having any

ideology or any talent.
But failure is an actual winning part.

Many well-known figures have experienced failure, which ultimately led them to their greatest successes. Here are some examples:

1.Thomas Edison: Famous for inventing the light bulb, Edison failed thousands of times before perfecting the technology.
He is quoted as saying, "I have not failed. I've just found 10,000 ways that won't work."

2.J.K. Rowling: The author of the Harry Potter series faced rejection from multiple publishers before her books became a global phenomenon.
She later said, "Failure is so important. It teaches you things you can't learn in success."

How to Handle Failure Effectively?

1.Change Your Perspective on Failure:

Instead of seeing failure as an endpoint, try viewing it as a temporary setback or a detour on the path to success. Reframing failure in a more positive light allows you to embrace it as part of the learning process.

Example: Instead of thinking, "I failed," try thinking, "I learned something important that will help me do better next time."

2.Reflect and Learn from the Experience:

Take time to reflect on the failure. What went wrong? What could you have done differently? What did you learn from the experience? Self-reflection helps you grow and avoid repeating the same mistakes in the future.
Example: If a business idea doesn't work, consider the reasons—whether it was the market, timing, product, or other factors. This analysis will inform your next steps.

3.Embrace the Emotions:

It's natural to feel disappointed, sad, or frustrated after failing, but don't let these emotions consume you. Acknowledge them and give yourself permission to feel, but don't stay stuck in negative emotions. Use your emotions as fuel to motivate yourself to try again with more insight and energy.
Example: Feeling upset about a personal failure is normal. After acknowledging your feelings, give yourself a timeframe to process them, then shift your focus toward constructive action.

It provides valuable lessons, fosters personal growth, and teaches resilience.
Rather than avoiding failure, we should learn to embrace it, understand its role in our development, and use it as a powerful tool for moving forward. Every failure offers an opportunity for learning, and with the right
mindset, it can propel you toward greater success and fulfillment.

CHAPTER SIX

STAGE-5 (PEER PRESSURE)

Peer pressure is a natural part of social life, and while it can lead to both positive and negative outcomes, it's crucial to be aware of its influence. Building self-confidence, setting clear values, and developing strong, supportive relationships can help individuals resist harmful peer pressure. At the same time, encouraging positive peer pressure in your social circles can create an environment where people feel empowered to make choices that benefit their well-being and personal growth.

refers to the influence exerted by a peer group on an individual to encourage them to adopt certain behaviors, attitudes, or actions. This influence can be either direct or subtle and can come from friends, classmates, coworkers, or even from society at large. While peer pressure is often thought of in a negative light—particularly when it leads someone to engage in risky or harmful behavior—it can also have positive effects, encouraging good habits or behaviors that align with social values.

Positive Peer Pressure: This occurs when peers encourage behaviors that are beneficial, such as studying hard, exercising, or participating in community service. Positive peer pressure can motivate individuals to grow, try new things, or engage in healthy behaviors.

Negative Peer Pressure: This involves peers urging someone to engage in behaviors that are harmful or risky, such as substance abuse, skipping school, or engaging in dangerous activities. Negative peer pressure is often the type most associated with problems like addiction, unhealthy habits, or risky behavior.

Why Peer Pressure is Powerful

Desire for Belonging: Humans are social creatures, and the desire to fit in or be accepted by others is a powerful motivator. Peer pressure capitalizes on this innate need for social belonging and approval.

Fear of Rejection: The fear of being excluded or rejected by a group can push people, particularly teenagers, to conform to group norms, even when those norms go against their better judgment or values.

Social Reinforcement: When a behavior is rewarded or encouraged by peers, it reinforces the idea that the behavior is acceptable or desirable. This can make someone more likely to continue the behavior, even if they initially had doubts.

The Role of Social Media and Peer Pressure

Social media has amplified peer pressure by providing a constant stream of comparisons and the desire for validation. On platforms like Instagram, TikTok, or Facebook, people are often exposed to curated images of others' lives, creating unrealistic standards of success, beauty, or happiness. This can lead to feelings of inadequacy or the pressure to conform to trends.

FOMO (Fear of Missing Out): Social media heightens the sense of FOMO, where individuals feel left out if they're not engaging in the same activities as their peers. This can lead people to make decisions based on the fear of being excluded rather than their own desires or well-being.

How to Resist Negative Peer Pressure

Set Clear Values and Boundaries: Establish what is important to you and what you stand for. When faced with peer pressure, knowing your values makes it easier to say no to behaviors that conflict with them.

Find Like-Minded People: Seek out friends or groups that share your values and interests. Positive peer influence can strengthen your ability to stand firm in your decisions.

Use Humor or Deflection: In some situations, you can deflect peer pressure using humor or lightheartedness. This can ease any tension and allow you to reject the pressure without confrontation.

Practice Self-Reflection: Take time to reflect on your choices and whether they align with your true desires and goals. Self-reflection strengthens personal growth and ensures you make decisions that support your long-term well-being.

#. How to Encourage Positive Peer Pressure

Be a Role Model: If you are in a position of influence, such as a friend, older sibling, or coworker, use your influence to promote positive behaviors. Encourage activities that promote health, personal growth, and well-being.

Support Healthy Choices: If you notice someone facing negative peer pressure, offer support and encouragement. Sometimes, simply offering an alternative or showing empathy can help someone feel empowered to make a healthier choice.

Create a Culture of Acceptance: Foster an environment where individuality is respected, and people are encouraged to make decisions based on their own beliefs, not just to fit in.

CHAPTER SEVEN

STAGE- 6(STRESS)

Stress in life is a common experience that can arise from various sources, both external and internal., whether these come from work, relationships, health, finances, or personal expectations. Stress is a natural reaction, but when it becomes chronic or overwhelming, it can negatively impact physical and mental health.

Causes of Stress:

1.Work and Career: High workloads, job insecurity, conflicts with coworkers, or unfulfilling jobs.

2.Relationships: Conflicts with family, friends, or romantic partners can contribute significantly to stress.

3.Financial Pressure: Money problems, debt, or concerns about financial stability can be a major source of stress.

4.Health Issues: Dealing with a serious illness, injury, or chronic health condition can trigger stress.

5.Life Changes: Major life events such as moving, changing jobs, or experiencing a loss can lead to heightened stress.

6.Personal Expectations: Feeling pressure to meet self-imposed standards of success or perfection.

Effects of Stress:

-Physical: Fatigue, headaches, muscle tension, digestive problems, and weakened immune function.

-Mental: Anxiety, depression, difficulty concentrating, mood swings, and feeling overwhelmed.

-Behavioral: Poor sleep, overeating or under-eating, procrastination, or avoiding important tasks.

Removing Strategies:

-Exercise: Physical activity can reduce stress hormones and increase endorphins, which boost mood.

-Mindfulness and Meditation: Practices like meditation, deep breathing, or yoga can help reduce stress and improve focus.

-Time Management: Prioritizing tasks, breaking them into smaller steps, and setting realistic goals can help reduce the feeling of being overwhelmed.

-Social Support: Talking with friends, family, or a counselor can help you process stress and feel supported.

-Healthy Lifestyle: A balanced diet, adequate sleep, and avoiding excessive alcohol or caffeine can improve your body's ability to manage stress.

Stress can evolve into depression when it becomes chronic and unaddressed, affecting both the mind and body in profound ways. While stress is a natural response to life's challenges, long-term or intense stress can overwhelm a person's coping mechanisms, eventually leading to depression.

Highly Impact on the Brain

Stress triggers the release of certain hormones, like cortisol, which help the body deal with immediate challenges. However, if the body is continuously under stress, cortisol levels remain elevated, and this can negatively affect brain regions that regulate mood. Chronic exposure to high levels of cortisol can damage these areas, impairing emotional regulation and contributing to feelings of sadness and hopelessness, which are hallmark symptoms of depression.

#Key Signs That Stress May Be Turning Into Depression:

-Persistent feelings of sadness or hopelessness that last for weeks or months.

-Loss of interest in activities that once brought joy or fulfillment.

-Difficulty concentrating or making decisions.

-Changes in sleep patterns (insomnia or excessive sleeping).

-Physical symptoms, such as unexplained aches, fatigue, or digestive problems, that don't improve.

-Withdrawal from social activities or relationships.

-Increased feelings of worthlessness or guilt.

-Thoughts of death or suicide.

#Prevention and Intervention:

It's crucial to address stress early to prevent it from developing into depression. Effective coping strategies such as mindfulness, exercise, and seeking social support can help prevent stress from overwhelming a person. If depression symptoms arise, seeking professional help from a therapist or counselor is important for treatment, as they can provide techniques to address both the underlying stress and depression itself.

CHAPTER EIGHT

STAGE -7(DEPRESSION)

Depression affects how a person thinks, feels, and behaves, and it can have significant physical, emotional, and psychological impacts.
While everyone experiences periods of low mood or sadness, depression is more than just feeling "down"

It can be triggered by various factors, and its exact cause can be complex.
But very common factors that can contribute to depression:

1.Psychological Factors:

Trauma or Stress: A history of trauma, abuse, or stressful life events (such as the loss of a loved one, divorce, or financial struggles) can trigger depression.

Low Self-Esteem: Negative self-talk, a critical inner voice, or a history of being undervalued can lead to depression.
Cognitive Patterns: Individuals who have a tendency toward negative thinking, rumination, or a pessimistic outlook may be more prone to depression.

2. Medical Conditions:

Certain medical conditions, such as chronic illness (e.g., diabetes, heart disease), cancer, or neurological disorders (e.g., Parkinson's disease), can contribute to or worsen depression.
Medications for other conditions (like corticosteroids or beta-blockers) may also have depression as a side effe
cts.

3.Environmental Factors:

Abuse or Neglect: Physical, emotional, or sexual abuse during childhood or adulthood can increse the risk of depression.

Improvement from depression ;-

Improving oneself from depression is a journey that

requires time, patience, and a multifaceted approach.
It involves not only seeking professional help when needed but also adopting personal strategies to promote emotional,
mental, and physical well-being. While depression can make even the simplest tasks feel overwhelming,
the good news is that there are many ways to support your recovery and improve your mental health.such as;-

1. *medication*
2. *taking therapy*
3. *sleep hygine*
4. *positive affirmations*

With the right tools, mindset, and support, you can take control of your depression and create a path toward a brighter, more fulfilling futur

CHAPTER NINE

STAGE -8 (WOUNDS)

Wounds in life refer to emotional, psychological, or even physical scars that result from painful experiences.
These wounds can stem from a variety of sources, such as trauma, loss, betrayal, rejection, failure, or difficult relationships.
They leave marks on our hearts and minds that can shape our beliefs, behaviors, and perceptions of the world.
Just as physical wounds require healing, emotional wounds also need attention, care, and time to heal.

Types of Wounds in Life:

1.Emotional Wounds:

-Rejection: Experiences of feeling unwanted or unloved, whether in relationships, friendships, or work, can leave deep emotional scars.
-Betrayal: Being hurt or deceived by someone you

trust—whether a partner, friend, or family member—can lead to feelings of deep pain and mistrust.
-Abandonment: The loss of a loved one, either through death, separation, or emotional distancing, can create a lasting feeling of emptiness.
-Inadequacy: Growing up with critical parents, bullying, or unrealistic expectations can lead to feelings of not being "good enough," affecting self-esteem.
-Failure: Experiencing failure or not achieving personal or professional goals can create a sense of disappointment, self-doubt, or shame.

2.Psychological Wounds:

-Trauma: This includes severe emotional or physical trauma, such as abuse, assault, or witnessing violence. Trauma often results in long-term psychological wounds, such as PTSD, anxiety, or depression.
-Guilt and Shame: Guilt over something you've done or failed to do can leave a lasting emotional scar, just as shame over perceived shortcomings or mistakes can make it hard to move forward.
-Fear: Fear of rejection, failure, or vulnerability can stem from past hurts, leading to avoidance of certain situations or people.
-Disappointment: Unmet expectations in life, whether in love, career, or personal achievement, can leave us feeling disillusioned or resigned.

3.Physical Wounds:

-Health Problems: Chronic illness, injury, or disability can create lasting physical pain, but also emotional or psychological struggles related to body image or limitations.
-Loss or Trauma: Loss of a physical capability due to an accident or illness, or the pain of chronic health issues, can deeply affect one's self-worth and outlook on life.

Wounds Taught as Teachers:

Although painful, life's wounds can also teach valuable lessons. They can make us more empathetic, resilient, and compassionate.
They can lead to a deeper understanding of ourselves, our needs, and the people around us. In many ways,
they shape who we become and how we navigate the world.

Example:

A person who has experienced deep loss may develop a greater appreciation for life and its fleeting beauty.
Someone who has faced rejection might develop a stronger sense of self-worth and resilience, learning to trust in their own value regardless of

external approval.

CHAPTER TEN

STAGE-9 (PATHS)

Navigating the Journey of Choices and Possibilities

Life is often compared to a journey, one that is uniquely our own, shaped by the choices we make, the challenges we face, and the lessons we learn. While the paths we walk may differ in their destinations, each path holds potential for growth, discovery, and transformation. The beauty of life lies not in the destination itself but in the journey—the experiences, moments, and decisions along the way.

The Path of Self-Discovery

The journey of self-discovery is one where you explore who you truly are, separate from the roles, labels, and expectations others may place on you. This path involves questioning your values, passions, and beliefs, and ultimately understanding what drives you. It can be challenging and uncomfortable, as it often means confronting parts of yourself that you may have ignored or suppressed.

The Path of Career and Ambition

The path of career is one of striving for success, building a professional identity, and achieving goals that give you a sense of accomplishment. This path is often marked by hard work, persistence, and the pursuit of excellence. Whether you're working your way up in a corporate job, building a business, or honing a craft, this path involves continuous learning, networking, and adaptability.

Key Elements:

Setting goals: Clear career goals provide direction and a sense of purpose.

Hard work: The willingness to put in effort and sacrifice in the pursuit of success.

Overcoming challenges: Navigating setbacks, failures, and rejections along the way.

The Reward: Professional success, financial stability, personal fulfillment, and a sense of accomplishment.

The Path of Healing and Inner Peace

Life's challenges often require us to heal—whether from past trauma, loss, or personal setbacks. The path of healing is about finding inner peace, emotional balance, and acceptance. This path is deeply personal and involves confronting pain, practicing self-care, and learning to embrace the present moment.

Key Elements:

Acceptance: Acknowledging and processing emotions rather than avoiding them.

Forgiveness: Letting go of resentment, both toward others and yourself.

Self-care: Prioritizing your mental, emotional, and physical well-being.

The Reward: Emotional healing, inner peace, and the ability to move forward with clarity and purpose.

CHAPTER ELEVEN

STAGE-10(HABIT)

Habits are the small, repeated actions or behaviors that, over time, have a profound impact on our lives. The importance of habits cannot be overstated because they shape who we are, how we feel, and the direction of our personal growth. In fact, much of what we do each day is governed by habits, many of which are formed unconsciously.

Building Positive Habits: A Few Tips

Start Small: Rather than trying to overhaul your entire routine, begin with one small habit. Focus on consistency and build gradually.

Make It Enjoyable: Choose habits that you genuinely enjoy or find meaningful. If it feels like a chore, you're less likely to stick with it.

Use Triggers: Attach your new habit to an existing routine. For example, after brushing your teeth, you might immediately meditate for 5 minutes. This "habit stacking" technique can help you remember and stick to new habits.

Track Your Progress: Keep track of your habits using an app, calendar, or journal. Tracking helps reinforce the habit and motivates you to keep going.

Be Patient: Habits take time to form—typically about 21 to 66 days, depending on the complexity of the habit. Be kind to yourself if you slip up, and keep going.

CHAPTER TWELVE

STAGE-11 (MOTIVATION)

Motivation is the spark that drives us to take action, push through challenges, and pursue our dreams. It's the force that pushes us to step outside our comfort zones, break through barriers, and keep going even when the path gets tough. Motivation can be both internal and external—driven by our desires, goals, values, and the people or circumstances around us. But ultimately, motivation comes from within. It's the inner fire that propels us forward when the world seems to push us back.

when you choose the great paths automatically motivation build inside your soul.

The Power to Keep Going

Motivation is like a fire—it can burn brightly for a while, but it requires constant fuel to keep going. You are the one who provides that fuel. By setting clear goals, embracing challenges, maintaining a positive environment, and staying disciplined, you can ignite and sustain the motivation necessary to achieve your dreams.

Remember, motivation is not a constant feeling—it comes and goes. But when you stay committed to your goals and push through even when motivation is low, you'll create momentum that will carry you through the toughest times. Keep going, stay focused on your "why," and believe in your ability to achieve what you set out to do.

You have everything within you to succeed. Keep the fire burning, and let it lead you to greatness.

CHAPTER THIRTEEN

STAGE -12 (HEALING)

Wounds in life are inevitable, but they do not define us.
Whether they are emotional, psychological, or physical, they all require time, patience, and care to heal.
Through self-awareness, self-compassion, and seeking support,
it's possible to recover and even find meaning in the experiences that once caused us pain.
Healing is not about erasing the past, but integrating it in a way that allows us to grow,
learn, and move forward stronger than before.

Healing an emotional or psychological wounds is a complex and ongoing process.
It requires patience, self-compassion, and often support from others.
The goal of healing is not to erase the past, but to integrate it in a way that allows you to move

forward without
it controlling or limiting you.

-Acknowledging the Pain: The first step in healing is recognizing and accepting that you have been hurt. Denying or suppressing the pain can prolong suffering. Acknowledging the wound allows you to process it instead of allowing it to fester and affect your life.

-Allowing Yourself to Feel: It's essential to allow yourself to experience and express the emotions related to the wound—whether sadness, anger, grief, or fear. Suppressing these feelings can lead to emotional numbness, depression, or anxiety.

-Self-Compassion and Forgiveness: Being kind and gentle with yourself is essential for healing. Self-compassion helps you accept that wounds are a natural part of life, and that making mistakes or experiencing pain doesn't make you weak or unworthy. Forgiveness—whether of yourself or others—can help release the hold that the wound has on you.

-Seeking Support: Healing from wounds is often easier when you have a support system. This could involve talking to trusted friends, family, or seeking professional help from a therapist or counselor. You don't have to carry the burden alone.

-Reframing the Narrative: How you perceive your wounds can either keep you stuck or set you free. Try to reframe your wounds as opportunities for growth or learning. For instance, a painful breakup might lead to a better understanding of what you need in a relationship, or a failure could teach resilience and the value of perseverance.

-Creating New Meaning: Many people find strength in creating new meaning from their wounds. This could involve helping others who have gone through similar pain, or using your experience to pursue a new passion, goal, or life direction. What seemed like a setback can sometimes become the foundation for a more purposeful, fulfilled life.

-Patience and Time: Healing is not instantaneous, and wounds often take longer to heal than we'd like. Giving yourself the time and space to heal without rushing the process is vital. Some days may feel like setbacks, but that's part of the journey.

-Letting Go: As you heal, it's essential to release what you can't control or change. This might mean letting go of resentment, fear, or anger that holds you back from moving forward. Letting go of the past doesn't mean forgetting—it means choosing to not let it dominate your present or future.

CHAPTER FOURTEEN

STAGE-13 (CHAKRAS)

Healing the chakras involves balancing and aligning the body's seven primary energy centers, which are believed to influence both physical and emotional health. In many spiritual and holistic healing traditions, particularly within practices like yoga and meditation, the chakras are considered to be energy hubs in the body that regulate various aspects of our life, including our health, emotions, relationships, and personal development.

Here's an overview of the 7 main chakras and how you can work on healing them:

1. Root Chakra (Muladhara)

Location: At the base of the spine, near the tailbone.

Element: Earth

Color: Red

Associated with: Safety, security, survival, basic needs (food, shelter, money).

Imbalance Symptoms: Feelings of insecurity, fear, anxiety, financial stress, instability, or physical issues with the legs, feet, or lower back.

Healing Practices:

Grounding exercises: Walking barefoot on earth or spending time in nature can help you reconnect with your root chakra.

Yoga poses: Mountain pose (Tadasana), Warrior poses (Virabhadrasana), and seated poses (Sukhasana).

Affirmations: "I am safe and secure." "I am grounded."

Use of red gemstones like garnet, ruby, or jasper can support the root chakra.

2. Sacral Chakra (Svadhisthana)

Location: Below the navel, in the pelvic area.

Element: Water

Color: Orange

Associated with: Creativity, pleasure, sensuality, emotions, relationships, and sexuality.

Imbalance Symptoms: Emotional instability, lack of creativity, sexual dysfunction, guilt, or difficulty with intimacy.

Healing Practices:

Water activities: Swimming, baths, or simply spending time near water can soothe the sacral chakra.

Yoga poses: Hip-opening poses like pigeon pose (Eka Pada Rajakapotasana) and butterfly pose (Baddha Konasana).

Affirmations: "I am open to experience pleasure." "I embrace my creativity and passion."

Use of orange gemstones like carnelian or orange calcite can support this chakra.

3. Solar Plexus Chakra (Manipura)

Location: Above the navel, in the stomach area.

Element: Fire

Color: Yellow

Associated with: Personal power, self-confidence, self-esteem, willpower, and the ability to take action.

Imbalance Symptoms: Low self-esteem, lack of direction, poor digestion, feeling powerless, or excessive control or aggression.

Healing Practices:

Solar plexus breathing exercises like diaphragmatic breathing or "fire breath" (Kapalbhati pranayama).

Yoga poses: Core-strengthening poses such as Boat pose (Navasana) and Warrior III (Virabhadrasana III).

Affirmations: "I trust myself and my abilities." "I am confident and empowered."

Use of yellow gemstones like citrine, amber, or tiger's eye can help balance the solar plexus.

4. Heart Chakra (Anahata)

Location: Center of the chest, near the heart.

Element: Air

Color: Green (sometimes pink)

Associated with: Love, compassion, empathy, forgiveness, emotional balance, and connection with others.

Imbalance Symptoms: Difficulty with relationships, inability to forgive, feelings of loneliness, or physical issues with the heart, lungs, or chest.

Healing Practices:

Heart-opening yoga poses like Camel pose (Ustrasana) and Cobra pose (Bhujangasana).

Breathing exercises: Practice slow, deep, and expansive breathing to open up the chest and encourage emotional release.

Affirmations: "I am love." "I open my heart to give and receive love freely."

Use of green gemstones like emerald, malachite, or rose quartz can nurture the heart chakra.

5. Throat Chakra (Vishuddha)

Location: Throat area.

Element: Ether (Space)

Color: Blue

Associated with: Communication, expression, truth, and creativity.

Imbalance Symptoms: Difficulty expressing yourself, fear of speaking up, sore throat, or tension in the neck and shoulders.

Healing Practices:

Chanting or mantras: Vocalizing mantras or singing can open the throat chakra.

Yoga poses: Fish pose (Matsyasana) and Shoulder stand (Sarvangasana).

Affirmations: "I speak my truth with confidence." "My voice matters."

Use of blue gemstones like lapis lazuli, turquoise, or aquamarine can support the throat chakra.

6. Third Eye Chakra (Ajna)

Location: Between the eyebrows, slightly above the bridge of the nose.

Element: Light

Color: Indigo or dark blue

Associated with: Intuition, insight, wisdom, perception, and spiritual awareness.

Imbalance Symptoms: Lack of clarity, feeling disconnected from intuition, headaches, or problems with vision or concentration.

Healing Practices:

Meditation: Practices that focus on the “mind’s eye,” visualization, or cultivating intuition.

Yoga poses: Child’s pose (Balasana) and forward bends (Uttanasana) to quiet the mind and stimulate the third eye.

Affirmations: "I trust my intuition." "I am connected to my inner wisdom."

Use of indigo gemstones like amethyst or sodalite can help balance the third eye chakra.

7. Crown Chakra (Sahasrara)

Location: Top of the head.

Element: Thought (Pure Consciousness)

Color: Violet or white

Associated with: Spiritual connection, enlightenment, universal consciousness, and connection to the divine.

Imbalance Symptoms: Feeling disconnected from spirituality, lack of purpose, apathy, or experiencing chronic headaches.

Healing Practices:

Meditation: Practices that focus on stillness, connection to the universe, and higher consciousness.

Yoga poses: Headstand (Sirsasana) or Lotus pose (Padmasana) to stimulate energy flow to the crown.

Affirmations: "I am connected to the divine." "I trust in the wisdom of the universe."

Use of violet or white gemstones like clear quartz, amethyst, or diamond can help activate the crown

chakra.

General Tips for Chakra Healing

Meditation: Regular meditation helps clear blockages and balance energy. You can focus on each chakra during your meditation, visualizing its associated color and imagining it spinning freely and harmoniously.

Breathing Exercises (Pranayama): Deep breathing and controlled breathwork can help move energy through the chakras, releasing tension and bringing balance.

Energy Healing (Reiki, Pranic Healing): Practitioners of energy healing can work to clear blockages and restore the flow of energy to the chakras.

Diet and Nutrition: Eating a balanced diet rich in fruits, vegetables, whole grains, and water can support your chakras. Each chakra is also associated with certain foods: root vegetables for the root chakra, citrus fruits for the solar plexus, leafy greens for the heart chakra, etc.

Sound Healing: Using sound frequencies (like singing bowls, chanting, or binaural beats) can help realign and restore the chakras to balance.

Healing and balancing your chakras can promote a sense of wholeness, emotional well-being, and physical vitality. While chakra healing practices are rooted in ancient spiritual traditions, they can be integrated into modern life through mindful practices like yoga, meditation, and energy healing. Regular attention to your chakras can help you cultivate greater self-awareness, reduce stress, and create a deeper connection to your body, mind, and spirit.

CHAPTER FIFTEEN

STAGE -14 (MEDITATION)

Meditation is a practice that involves focusing the mind and calming the body in order to achieve a state of mental clarity,
emotional balance, and physical relaxation. Meditation offers numerous benefits and can play a transformative role in daily life.
By cultivating mindfulness and awareness, meditation helps individuals reconnect with the present
moment and gain a deeper understanding of their thoughts, emotions, and behaviors.

This reduces the physical effects of stress, such as high blood pressure and increased heart rate.the practice of paying full attention
to your thoughts, feelings, and bodily sensations without judgment. This heightened awareness helps you understand your emotions,

triggers, and reactions, leading to greater emotional intelligence.Meditation offers a way to process unresolved emotions from past experiences,

traumas, or wounds. It allows you to observe these emotions from a place of detachment, which can reduce their emotional grip on you.

Incorporating Meditation into Daily Life;-

Here are some tips for doing so:

-Start Small: If you're new to meditation, start with just 5–10 minutes a day.
Gradually increase the duration as you become more comfortable with the practice.

-Set a Routine: Try to meditate at the same time each day, whether in the morning, during lunch, or before bed. Consistency is key to forming a habit.

-Create a Calm Space: Find a quiet, comfortable spot where you won't be disturbed. This could be a corner in your room, a park bench, or even your car.

-Focus on Your Breath: Breathing is a simple but powerful anchor for meditation. Focus on the sensation of your breath coming in and out. When your mind wanders (which it will), gently bring

your focus back to the breath.

to reduce stress, improve your health, enhance your relationships, or connect more deeply with your inner self, meditation
offers a simple yet profound tool for transformation.

CHAPTER SIXTEEN

STAGE - 15 (SPIRITUALITY)

It refers to the deep, personal journey of exploring and understanding one's connection to something greater than oneself,
whether it's a higher power, the universe, nature, or the inner self.
It encompasses practices, beliefs, and experiences that guide individuals toward meaning, purpose, and inner peace.
While spirituality is often associated with religion, it is a broader concept that can be
independent of any formal religious tradition, focusing instead on personal growth, the search for truth, and the
cultivation of compassion and love.

Spirituality can be cultivated through various practices that nourish the mind, body, and soul.
The practices may vary greatly depending on one's belief system, but some common approache include:

1.Prayer:

Prayer is a common practice in many religious traditions, where individuals communicate with the divine,
seeking guidance, strength, or expressing gratitude. Even for those not affiliated with a specific religion, prayer or intention-setting can be a powerful way to center the mind and spirit.

Spirituality vs. Religion:

While spirituality and religion are often intertwined, they are not synonymous.
Religion typically involves organized practices, doctrines, and institutions centered around worship and belief in a higher power.
Spirituality, on the other hand, is more individual and personal, focusing on the direct experience of connection and meaning.
One can be spiritual without adhering to a specific religion, and one can also practice spirituality within the framework of a religious tradition.

The Role of Spirituality i our Daily Life:

1.Navigating Challenges:

Spirituality can provide the strength and perspective needed to cope with life's difficulties, such as illness, loss, or personal crises. It offers a framework to understand suffering and find meaning in hardship.
-Example: Viewing challenges as opportunities for growth, and trusting that everything happens for a reason, can help you endure tough times with grace.

2.Fostering Gratitude:

A spiritual practice often emphasizes the importance of gratitude—appreciating life's blessings, both big and small. Gratitude shifts focus from what's lacking to what's present, enhancing overall happiness and satisfaction.
-Example: Taking time each day to reflect on what you're grateful for, cultivating an attitude of thankfulness and joy.

3.Cultivating Inner Peace:

Spirituality offers tools for achieving peace of mind, reducing stress, and fostering emotional balance. By practicing mindfulness or meditation, you can create a sense of calm and balance, regardless of external circumstances.
-Example: Taking a few moments to meditate before starting your day, helping to center your mind and approach your tasks with a calm and

focused mindset.

4.Nurturing Relationships:

Spirituality often emphasizes the importance of love, compassion, and respect in relationships. Cultivating these qualities leads to healthier, more meaningful connections with others.
-Example: Approaching relationships with empathy, forgiveness, and kindness, creating deeper emotional bonds and harmonious connections.

CHAPTER SEVENTEEN

STAGE - 16(IMPROVEMENT)

Improvement in life is a continual journey rather than a destination. It involves small, intentional changes that gradually elevate our mindset, behaviors, and overall well-being. Life doesn't improve overnight, but with consistent effort, we can transform ourselves and our circumstances. The key lies in embracing growth and making deliberate choices that align with our highest potential.

1.Developing Healthy Habits

Our habits define our lives. Positive habits support personal growth and well-being, while negative ones hinder progress. Identifying and cultivating good habits can have a profound impact on your life.

How to improve:

Prioritize healthy habits like regular exercise, balanced nutrition, and adequate sleep.

Cultivate mental habits such as gratitude, mindfulness, and positive self-talk.

Replace detrimental habits (e.g., procrastination, negative thinking) with productive alternatives.

2. Building Resilience

Life will inevitably throw challenges your way, but how you respond to adversity is what matters most. Building resilience is essential for maintaining progress, even when things get tough.

How to improve:

Embrace challenges as opportunities for growth rather than setbacks.

Cultivate mental toughness by practicing stress management techniques.

Surround yourself with supportive people who uplift and encourage you during tough times.

3. Taking Responsibility

Improvement in life comes from taking full responsibility for your actions, choices, and circumstances. When you stop blaming others or external factors, you regain the power to change your situation.

How to improve:

Own your mistakes and learn from them.

Take proactive steps to correct things that aren't working in your life.

Accept that you are in control of your decisions and actions, even when life feels uncertain.

4. Cultivating Positive Relationships

Our relationships profoundly affect our happiness and success. Surround yourself with people who inspire, challenge, and support you. Positive relationships act as a foundation for personal growth.

How to improve:

Spend time with people who encourage your growth and bring positivity into your life.

Practice empathy, active listening, and open communication in your relationships.

Set boundaries to protect your energy and prioritize those who align with your values.

5. Embracing Change

Life is ever-changing, and growth often requires us to adapt. Embracing change means being flexible and willing to evolve with the circumstances rather than resisting them.

How to improve:

See change as an opportunity to improve, rather than a threat.

Stay open to new experiences and be willing to step out of your comfort zone.

Trust that change can lead to better opportunities and personal growth.

6. Nurturing a Growth Mindset

A growth mindset is the belief that abilities and intelligence can be developed through effort, learning, and perseverance. Cultivating this mindset can dramatically enhance your ability to improve.

How to improve:

View setbacks as opportunities to learn, not as failures.

Celebrate your progress, no matter how small.

Practice self-compassion and avoid harsh self-criticism when things don't go as planned.

7. Living with Purpose

Having a sense of purpose brings direction and meaning to your life. When you live with intention, your actions align with your values and vision, making improvement more fulfilling and impactful.

How to improve:

Reflect on what truly matters to you and set goals aligned with your values.

Focus on contributing to others, whether through your work, relationships, or community.

Cultivate a sense of gratitude for the present moment, while remaining focused on the future.

Improvement in life isn't about perfection—it's about progress. It's about making small, intentional changes every day that, over time, add up to a transformation.

It's about understanding that the path to becoming the best version of yourself is not linear; there will be setbacks, but they are part of the process. The key is to keep moving forward, no matter the pace.

Remember that the most significant improvements often come not from big, dramatic shifts but from consistent, daily actions. By embracing self-awareness, continuous learning, and resilience, you create a foundation for a life that grows stronger, richer, and more fulfilling with each passing day.

You have the power to shape your life. Start today, and watch as you transform your future one small step at a time.

CHAPTER EIGHTEEN

STAGE-17(HAPPINESS)

happiness is a journey rather than a fixed destination. It's about cultivating positive habits, building strong connections, and making choices that align with your values and desires. It's perfectly normal for happiness to ebb and flow, but by focusing on these elements, you can increase your capacity to experience joy, meaning, and fulfillment in life.

Happiness in life is one of those things that seems simple yet complex. It can mean different things to different people, but there are a few common threads that often come up when people reflect on what makes life fulfilling and joyful.

Happiness in life is a multifaceted experience, shaped by various elements that can enhance or hinder our sense of well-being. While it can be deeply personal, there are some common aspects that contribute to a fulfilling and joyful life. Here's a breakdown of key aspects of happiness in life:

1. Positive Relationships

Why it matters: Social connections are among the strongest predictors of happiness. The bonds we share with family, friends, and partners provide emotional support, companionship, and a sense of belonging.

How to cultivate it: Focus on quality over quantity in your relationships. Nurture existing friendships, prioritize time with loved ones, and seek to build new connections with people who share your values.

2. Meaning and Purpose

Why it matters: A sense of purpose brings direction to life and can make even challenging situations feel worthwhile. Having a reason to get out of bed each morning provides a framework for making decisions, setting goals, and finding motivation.

How to cultivate it: Identify what feels meaningful to you—whether it's through work, volunteering, personal projects, or family. Pursue passions or causes that align with your values and create a sense of contribution.

3. Gratitude

Why it matters: Gratitude shifts our focus from what's lacking to what we already have, increasing our appreciation for life. People who practice gratitude tend to have higher levels of well-being, reduced stress, and better physical health.

How to cultivate it: Keep a gratitude journal, where you write down a few things you're grateful for each day. Take time to savor the good moments, even small ones, and remind yourself regularly of what you appreciate in life.

4. Self-Acceptance

Why it matters: Accepting yourself—flaws and all—promotes inner peace and reduces negative self-talk. People who practice self-compassion are less likely to engage in harmful comparisons or hold themselves to unrealistic standards.

How to cultivate it: Practice self-compassion by being gentle with yourself in moments of failure or difficulty. Celebrate your strengths, learn from your mistakes, and embrace your authentic self.

5. Mindfulness and Presence

Why it matters: Happiness often resides in the present moment, not in the past or future. Mindfulness helps us savor life as it unfolds and reduces stress by preventing us from ruminating on what's already happened or worrying about what's to come.

How to cultivate it: Engage in mindfulness practices like meditation, deep breathing, or simply paying attention to your senses. Take moments throughout the day to be fully present in what you're doing, whether it's eating, walking, or conversing with someone.

Happiness isn't a single destination but a collection of experiences, mindsets, and practices. The combination of these aspects varies from person to person, but integrating more of these elements into your life can contribute to greater fulfillment, joy, and a deeper sense of meaning.

CHAPTER NINETEEN

STAGE -18(CALMNESS)

With emotional resilience, mental clarity, and a sense of control over one's reactions.
It's about maintaining a balanced state of mind, free from excessive worry, fear, or agitation.
Cultivating calmness is essential for both mental well-being and the ability to make sound decisions in difficult circumstances.

Calmness is not something that can be forced or attained instantly, but through consistent practice, it is possible to cultivate a deep sense of peace and inner stability. It requires developing tools that help you manage stress, emotions, and external pressures with grace and clarity.

In a world that often prioritizes speed, productivity, and external achievement, calmness is a form of emotional mastery. It allows you to navigate life's ups and downs with grace, clarity, and a sense of inner stillness. Calmness can enhance mental and physical well-being, reduce stress, and improve relationships, making it a highly valuable quality to develop.

How to Cultivate Calmness in Life?

Achieving calmness is a lifelong practice that requires patience, consistency, and self-awareness. Here are some practical ways to cultivate calmness and integrate it into your everyday life:

1. Mindfulness and Meditation
Mindfulness is the practice of paying attention to the present moment with awareness and without judgment. Meditation helps to center the mind and release mental clutter, allowing for a deeper sense of calmness.

How to Practice: Start with just a few minutes of mindfulness each day. Sit quietly, focus on your breath, and gently bring your attention back to the present whenever your mind starts to wander.
Benefits: Meditation trains your mind to be present, reduces rumination, and cultivates a sense of peace that extends into everyday life.

2. Breathing Techniques
Deep breathing is a simple yet powerful way to activate the body's relaxation response. When you're feeling stressed or overwhelmed, focusing on your breath can help restore calm.

Deep Breathing: Practice slow, deep inhales and exhales, ideally breathing in for a count of 4, holding for 4, and exhaling for 4. This calms the nervous system and helps you regain emotional balance.
Box Breathing: A technique where you inhale for 4 counts, hold for 4, exhale for 4, and
hold again for 4 counts. This can help reduce anxiety and increase focus.

3. Create a Calming Environment
The environment around you significantly influences your mental state. A peaceful, organized space promotes calmness, while clutter and chaos can create stress.

Declutter Your Space: Organize your living or working environment to create a sense of order and simplicity. A tidy space often leads to a clearer mind.
Use Calming Elements: Surround yourself with soothing colors (like soft blues or greens), pleasant scents
(such as lavender or sandalwood), and calming sounds (like soft music or nature sounds).

4. Practice Acceptance
One of the most powerful ways to cultivate calmness is to accept things as they are. Instead of resisting what you cannot change or constantly striving for an idealized version of life, embrace the present moment and all that comes with it.

Let Go of Control: Focus on what you can control—your actions, responses, and attitude—while accepting that some things are beyond your control.
Embrace Imperfection: Life is messy, unpredictable, and imperfect. Rather than stressing over everything that's wrong, practice self-compassion and learn to embrace imperfections as part of the human experience.

5. Develop Emotional Resilience
Emotional resilience is the ability to recover quickly from setbacks and handle life's challenges without being overwhelmed. Calmness is a key component of emotional resilience.

Self-Awareness: Recognize when you're feeling stressed, anxious, or overwhelmed. This awareness is the first step to managing those emotions in a healthy way.
Self-Compassion: Be kind to yourself during difficult moments. Understand that it's okay to feel emotions like sadness, frustration, or anger, but don't let those emotions control your reactions.

Reframe Negative Thoughts: Practice replacing negative, reactive thoughts with more balanced, positive ones. For example, instead of thinking "I can't handle this," think "This is difficult, but I can take it one step at a time."

6. Spend Time in Nature
Nature has a natural calming effect. Whether it's a walk in the park, hiking in the mountains, or simply sitting near a body of water, time outdoors can help restore balance and bring a sense of peace.

Nature Walks: Take regular walks in natural environments. Use these moments to clear your mind and reconnect with the natural world.
Mindful Presence: Practice mindfulness while outdoors by paying attention to the sounds, sights, and smells around you. Nature
can help you ground yourself in the present moment.

CHAPTER TWENTY

STAGE -19 (WINNING LIFE LIKE A WARRIOR)

Being a "warrior" in life doesn't mean physical combat, but rather fighting for your dreams,
defending your values, and winning in your personal growth, goals, and relationships.
It's about cultivating inner strength, mastering your emotions, and living with purpose and integrity.

Winning life as a warrior is about strength, resilience, discipline, and living with honor and purpose. It's not about avoiding difficulty, but about embracing challenges as opportunities to grow, learn, and evolve into the best version of yourself. The warrior spirit is one of inner mastery, emotional control, and unwavering commitment to living a life of integrity, passion, and service to what matters most.

To live like a warrior, you must prepare daily—through physical training, mental discipline, emotional
resilience, and a clear sense of purpose. Whether you're facing personal struggles, professional challenges,
or emotional battles, the warrior mindset equips you with the tools to overcome adversity and achieve greatness,
both within yourself and in the world around you.

Short note for success;-

Success in life is a holistic concept that includes personal achievement, happiness, fulfillment, meaningful relationships, health, and making a positive impact. It's about aligning your actions with your core values, learning from your experiences, and staying persistent in the face of challenges. True success is not just about external

accomplishments—it's about living a life that is purposeful, balanced, and fulfilling in all aspects.

Focus on personal growth, build resilience, develop strong relationships, and make a meaningful contribution to the world around you. Ultimately, success in life is about becoming the best version of yourself and living in alignment with your values, passions, and purpose.

thank You Note For Readers

Dear Readers,

Thank you for taking the time to engage with this content. Your curiosity and willingness to explore these ideas mean a lot. Life is a journey, and the path to growth, peace, and strength is often full of challenges, but it's also filled with opportunities. I hope the words here have provided inspiration, clarity, and encouragement for you to face whatever battles you may be experiencing in your own life.

Remember, every step forward—no matter how small—is progress. Keep your heart strong, your mind clear, and your spirit unwavering. I'm grateful to be part of your journey, and I hope you continue to grow, learn, and win in every aspect of your life.

Stay strong and keep pushing forward. You have everything within you to live a life of purpose and power.

With gratitude,
[SANANSHIKA MALIK]

Feedback

I hope you enjoyed reading my book! I'd love to hear your thoughts—what worked well for you, and any suggestions you might have. Your feedback is invaluable as I continue to grow as a writer. Thank you so much for taking the time to share!"

SCAN TO GIVE FEEDBACK AND TO KNOW MORE DETAILS OF BOOK EVENTS AND LAUNCHING.

www.ingramcontent.com/pod-product-compliance
Lightning Source LLC
LaVergne TN
LVHW041046150826
845672LV00001B/494